W9-DDX-725

Fahrenheit, Celsius, and Their Temperature Scales

Yoming S. Lin

PowerKiDS press.

New York

In memory of Grandpa Tin-mo, an inventor and true Renaissance Man

Published in 2012 by The Rosen Publishing Group, Inc.
29 East 21st Street, New York, NY 10010

First Edition

Editor: Amelie von Zumbusch
Book Design: Greg Tucker

Photo Credits: Cover (Anders Celsius), p. 20 (top right) Uppsala University Art Collections; cover (Daniel Gabriel Fahrenheit), p. 20 (top left) by Gregory Tucker; cover (thermometer), pp. 4, 5 (top, bottom), 6, 7, 8, 9 (bottom), 10, 11 (top, bottom), 13, 15, 16, 17, 21 (top, bottom) Shutterstock.com; pp. 9 (top), 12 iStockphoto/Thinkstock; p. 14 BananaStock/Thinkstock; p. 18 Science & Society Picture Library/Getty Images; p. 19 © www.iStockphoto.com/gradts; p. 20 Pierre-Denis Martin/The Bridgeman Art Library/Getty Images.

Library of Congress Cataloging-in-Publication Data

Lin, Yoming S.
 Fahrenheit, Celsius, and their temperature scales / by Yoming S. Lin. — 1st ed.
     p. cm. — (Eureka!)
 Includes index.
 ISBN 978-1-4488-5035-8 (library binding)
 1. Temperature measurements—Juvenile literature. 2. Thermometers—Juvenile literature. I. Title.
 QC271.4.L56 2012
 536'.50287—dc22
                          2011008175

Manufactured in the United States of America

CPSIA Compliance Information: Batch #WS11PK: For Further Information contact Rosen Publishing, New York, New York at 1-800-237-9932

Contents

Two Scientists

Temperature is a measurement of how hot or cold something is. Knowing the temperature outside helps us know what to wear. Doctors check our body temperatures to see if we are healthy. Two scientists who lived hundreds of years ago made these things possible.

This thermometer uses both the Fahrenheit scale and the Celsius scale. "Fahrenheit" is often shortened to F, while "Celsius" becomes C. The symbol ° stands for "degrees."

Daniel Gabriel Fahrenheit invented a **thermometer** that was better than earlier ones. A thermometer is a tool that is used to read temperatures. He also created the first widely used temperature scale, or standard set of numbers used for measuring temperatures. Anders Celsius created another temperature scale. This is the scale that scientists use today. Fahrenheit and Celsius will always be remembered for their important work.

Top: Sick people often have fevers, or body temperatures that are too high. *Bottom*: There are many kinds of thermometers. Meat thermometers like this one are used in cooking.

Young Fahrenheit

Daniel Gabriel Fahrenheit was born on May 24, 1686. He was born in Gdańsk, a city in what is now Poland. His parents were Daniel and Concordia Fahrenheit. Sadly, both his parents died from eating poisonous mushrooms when he was just 15 years old.

Fahrenheit then started training to become a merchant in Amsterdam,

This is Gdańsk, the city where Fahrenheit was born. The city is a port on the Baltic Sea, in northern Europe. It has been a center for trading goods for hundreds of years.

Amsterdam, seen here, is known for its canals. These are man-made waterways. Amsterdam has a long history as an important city for merchants.

in the Netherlands. There, he learned about the first modern thermometers. These were being made in Florence, Italy. Fahrenheit was curious about the thermometers. He soon decided that he was not interested in becoming a merchant. He left his training and traveled to many cities. He learned new things in each place.

The Glass Thermometer

Fahrenheit settled in The Hague, in the Netherlands. He became a **glassblower**, or person who makes things out of glass. One thing he made was thermometers.

His earliest thermometers were glass tubes with **alcohol**, a liquid, at the bottom of the tubes. As it got warmer,

These men are blowing glass. Glassblowers blow into long pipes to shape objects out of melted glass.

the alcohol took up more space and rose in the tube.

These thermometers were not very useful because they were all different. Each one would give different readings even if they were all measuring the same thing. They were helpful only in showing temperature changes. Fahrenheit wanted to create standard thermometers. That way, if a thermometer read 50 **degrees**, everyone would know what that meant.

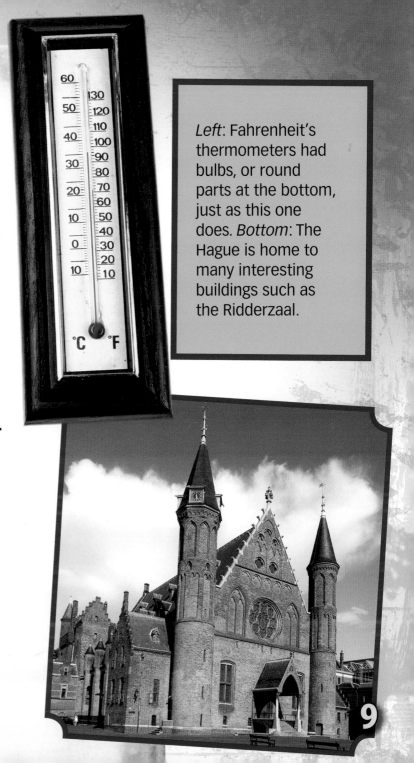

Left: Fahrenheit's thermometers had bulbs, or round parts at the bottom, just as this one does. *Bottom*: The Hague is home to many interesting buildings such as the Ridderzaal.

9

Fahrenheit used his glassblowing skills to make thin tubes that worked well in thermometers. Next, he created a temperature scale. He made the coldest mix of salt, ice, and water he could. He called the level that the alcohol reached when

Mercury, seen here, is a shiny, silver-colored metal. It is one of only a few metals that are liquid at room temperature.

the thermometer was placed in this mix 0. He decided that the temperature of the human body would be 96. He broke the space in between into 96 equal degrees.

Later, Fahrenheit used liquid **mercury** instead of alcohol. Mercury rises at a slower, steadier rate than alcohol. This made the thermometer easier to read. He also changed his scale so there would be 180 degrees between boiling water and freezing water.

Top: Healthy people's bodies are all around the same temperature. *Bottom*: Fahrenheit died in 1686. He was buried in The Hague's Kloosterkerk, seen here.

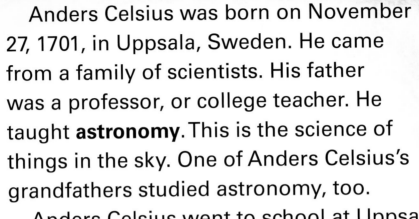

Anders Celsius was born on November 27, 1701, in Uppsala, Sweden. He came from a family of scientists. His father was a professor, or college teacher. He taught **astronomy**. This is the science of things in the sky. One of Anders Celsius's grandfathers studied astronomy, too.

Anders Celsius went to school at Uppsala University. After he was done with his studies, he became an astronomy professor there. His

Uppsala, Sweden, is known for its cathedral, seen here. The city is also home to Scandinavia's oldest university, Uppsala University.

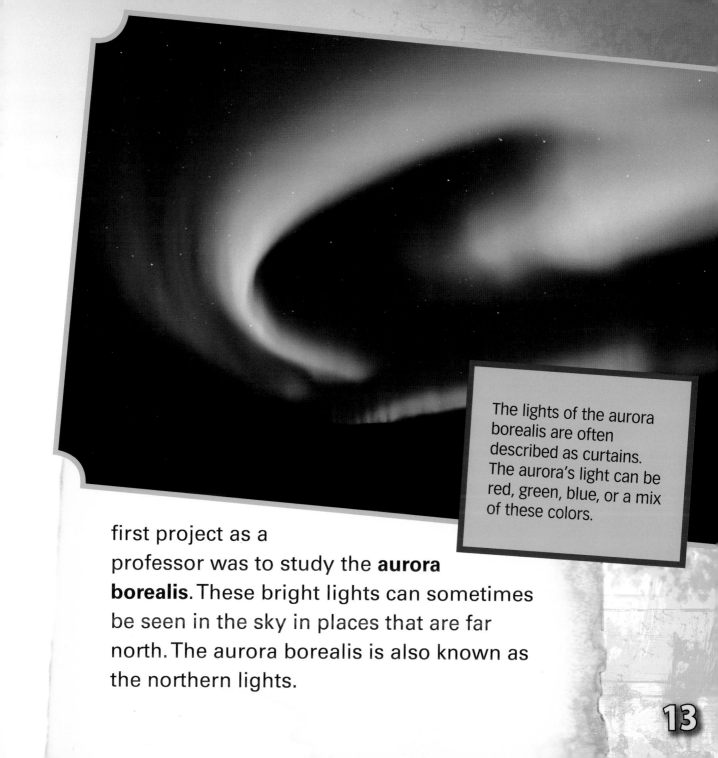

The lights of the aurora borealis are often described as curtains. The aurora's light can be red, green, blue, or a mix of these colors.

first project as a professor was to study the **aurora borealis**. These bright lights can sometimes be seen in the sky in places that are far north. The aurora borealis is also known as the northern lights.

Celsius's Early Work

Celsius discovered that the aurora borealis is related to Earth's **magnetic field**. Earth acts like a huge magnet. Its magnetic field is the area around Earth where its magnetism can be felt. Earth's magnetic field makes **particles**, or tiny pieces, from the Sun move toward Earth's **magnetic poles**, or magnetic ends. These particles crash into particles in the **atmosphere**, or air

Earth's magnetic field makes a compass's needle point north. Since compass needles always point north, people can use them to figure out what direction they are facing.

Lapland is the northernmost part of mainland Europe. It is the homeland of the Sami people. It is very snowy and is known for its reindeer.

around Earth. This causes the lights.

Celsius also traveled with a group of scientists to Lapland. They measured the length between one **meridian** and the next. Meridians are imaginary lines that connect Earth's northernmost and southernmost points. Scientists break Earth into 360 evenly spaced meridians. The scientists' measurements gave clues to Earth's shape.

Celsius Makes a Scale

Celsius also came up with a temperature scale that was easier to use than Fahrenheit's. He set the freezing point of water at 100 degrees. He used the boiling point of water as the 0-degree mark. He separated the thermometer into 100 degrees.

Celsius did many tests on the freezing and boiling points of water, too. His tests showed

Freshwater freezes at 0 degrees on the version of the Celsius scale used now. Seawater, like the water that formed this iceberg, freezes at an even colder temperature.

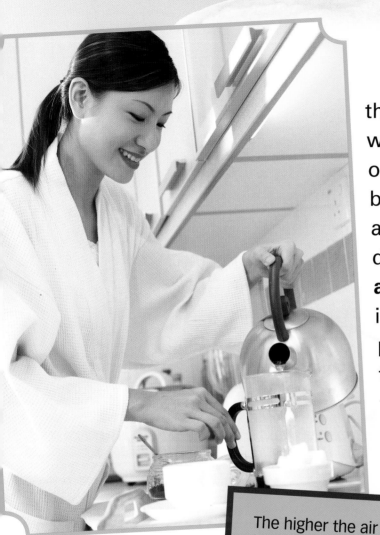

that the freezing point of water is the same everywhere on Earth. He found that the boiling point of water is not always the same. It changes depending on a place's **atmospheric pressure**. This is how hard the air above presses down. Celsius used this information to make thermometers that worked correctly everywhere.

The higher the air pressure is, the higher the temperature water will boil at will be. Air pressure changes with the weather. Air pressure drops as you move above sea level, too.

After Celsius died, another scientist changed his scale so that water's freezing point became 0 degrees and its boiling point became 100 degrees. Today, the Celsius scale is used in most countries. In the United States, we use the Celsius scale in science. We use Fahrenheit's scale for the weather.

Modern scientists also use the Kelvin scale. William Thompson, who was also called

Lord Kelvin was a British scientist who lived from 1824 to 1907. He discovered absolute zero, the coldest possible temperature. Absolute zero is $-273.15°$ C and $-459.67°$ F.

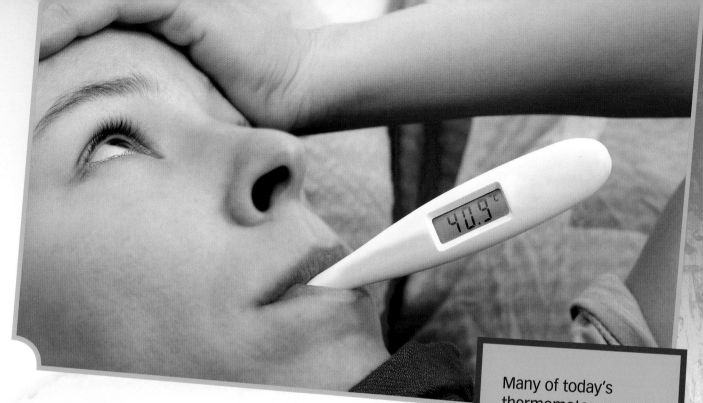

Lord Kelvin, came up with this temperature scale. On it, 0 degrees is the coldest temperature possible.

Fahrenheit and Celsius will always be remembered for what they gave to science. They made reading temperatures possible, everywhere from the lab to the kitchen to the playground.

Many of today's thermometers are digital thermometers, such as the one this sick woman is using. As you can see, the thermometer here uses the Celsius scale.

Timeline

Fahrenheit

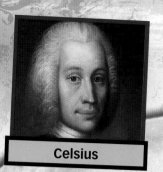

Celsius

The calendars people use have changed over time. The dates here are from the calendars that were in use when and where these events happened.

May 24, 1686

Daniel Gabriel Fahrenheit is born in Gdańsk, in what is now Poland.

1714

Fahrenheit invents his mercury thermometer in The Hague, in the Netherlands.

February 17, 1720

The Treaty of The Hague is signed at The Hague. This ended a war between Spain and Great Britain, France, Austria, and the Dutch Republic.

1660   1670   1680   1690   1700   1710

1700

The Great Northern War starts between Sweden and Russia. Many countries in Europe are part of this war.

November 27, 1701

Anders Celsius is born in Uppsala, Sweden.

20

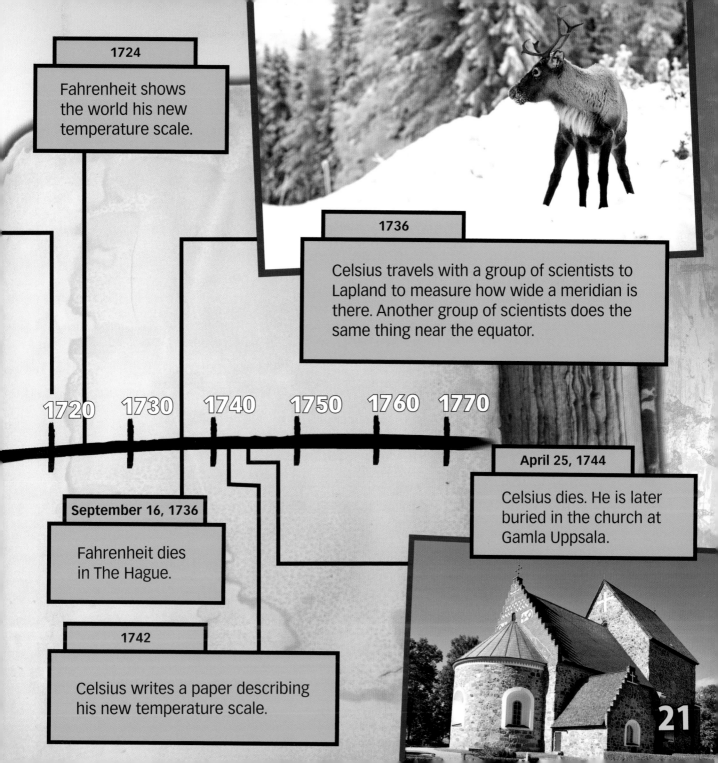

1724

Fahrenheit shows the world his new temperature scale.

1736

Celsius travels with a group of scientists to Lapland to measure how wide a meridian is there. Another group of scientists does the same thing near the equator.

1720　1730　1740　1750　1760　1770

April 25, 1744

Celsius dies. He is later buried in the church at Gamla Uppsala.

September 16, 1736

Fahrenheit dies in The Hague.

1742

Celsius writes a paper describing his new temperature scale.

Inside the Science

1. Fahrenheit made a thermometer that was better than earlier ones. He made thin glass tubes that were equally wide from top to bottom. This let the liquid rise at a steady rate.

2. Fahrenheit's mercury thermometers worked well. However, modern thermometers used for taking people's temperatures almost never use mercury. This is because we now know that mercury can make people sick. Mercury is still sometimes used in weather thermometers, though.

3. Celsius did many tests to show that the boiling point of water depends on atmospheric pressure. He found that when the atmospheric pressure is lower, the boiling point of water is lower, too.

4. The Celsius scale has 100 degrees between the freezing point of water and its boiling point at a certain atmospheric pressure. This 100-degree system is easy to understand and remember.

5. Celsius and other scientists measured the length between one meridian and the next meridian in different places. Their work gave clues to the shape of Earth. It showed that Earth is round with flattened North and South Poles.

Glossary

alcohol (AL-kuh-hol) A clear liquid that pours and burns easily.

astronomy (uh-STRAH-nuh-mee) The science of the Sun, the Moon, planets, and stars.

atmosphere (AT-muh-sfeer) The gases around an object in space. On Earth this is air.

atmospheric pressure (at-muh-SFEER-ik PREH-shur) The weight of the air pressing down on something.

aurora borealis (uh-RAWR-uh bawr-ee-A-lus) Bands of often colorful light that sometimes occur in the night sky in northern parts of the world.

degrees (dih-GREEZ) Measurements of how hot or cold something is.

glassblower (GLAS-bloh-er) A person who makes things out of glass.

magnetic field (mag-NEH-tik FEELD) The area around a magnet where its pull is felt.

magnetic poles (mag-NEH-tik POHLZ) The areas of a magnet where the force of magnetism is strongest.

mercury (MER-kyuh-ree) A poisonous, silver-colored element.

meridian (meh-RIH-dee-un) One of the imaginary lines that run north and south and break Earth into 360 equal parts.

particles (PAR-tih-kulz) Small pieces of something.

temperature (TEM-pur-cher) How hot or cold something is.

thermometer (ther-MAH-meh-ter) A tool used to measure temperature.

Index

Web Sites

Due to the changing nature of Internet links, PowerKids Press has developed an online list of Web sites related to the subject of this book. This site is updated regularly. Please use this link to access the list:
www.powerkidslinks.com/eure/fahrenheit/